LOS ANGELES

ALSO BY AMY UYEMATSU

Basic Vocabulary
The Yellow Door
Stone Bow Prayer
Nights of Fire, Nights of Rain
30 Miles from J-Town

THAT BLUE TRICKSTER TIME

THAT BLUE TRICKSTER TIME

AMY UYEMATSU

LOS ANGELES

Copyright © 2022 by Amy Uyematsu. All rights reserved.
Published in the United States by What Books Press,
the imprint of the Glass Table Collective, Los Angeles.

Library of Congress Cataloging-in-Publication Data

Names: Uyematsu, Amy, author.
Title: That blue trickster time / Amy Uyematsu.
Description: Los Angeles : What Books Press, [2022] | Summary:
  "In *That Blue Trickster Time*, Amy Uyematsu addresses her life as an older
  Japanese American woman—rooted in the ancestral wisdom of goddess and
  stones, her poems confront contemporary issues of racism, pandemic
  uncertainty and political justice."— Provided by publisher.
Identifiers: LCCN 2022002151 | ISBN 9780996227698 (paperback)
Subjects: LCGFT: Poetry.
Classification: LCC PS3571.Y66 T48 2022 | DDC 811/.54--dc23/eng/20220118
LC record available at https://lccn.loc.gov/2022002151

Cover art: Gronk, *Untitled*, mixed media on paper, 2021
Book design by Ash Good, www.ashgood.com

What Books Press
363 South Topanga Canyon Boulevard
Topanga, CA 90290

WHATBOOKSPRESS.COM

to
my husband Raúl

CONTENTS

PART I

Guanyin, Goddess of Mercy	3
Elder Sister	4
Among the Containers	6
Shamisen & Straw	9
The Basket	11
Comfort Women	13
None of These Women Are Smiling	15
Sister Muse	17
It Isn't Coincidence	18
An Afternoon with Guitar Shorty	19
Zumba Gold at 9 AM	20
& My Five Desires	21
This Hand	23
Ancestral Sentries	24
The Older, The More	25

PART II

36 Views of Manzanar	33
The Bachi-Bachi Buddhahead Blues	51
So Are We Becoming More Visible	53
Pandemic Postscript: Or Are We Too Visible Again	56
I Wish I'd Seen My Nisei Father Dance	57
The Suitcase	59
Little Tokyo Haiku, 2019	61
Love-In for Jeremy Lin	62
How To Become a Better Noodle Poet	63
Dear Lawson	64
Sister Stone	69

PART III

This Tree, That Tree	73
When the World Agrees on Nothing	74
Winter, 2016	75
The Panthers	76
American Summer: 8 Tanka	77
Unrelenting This Heat / Unforgiving This July	79
Chinese Snowballs at Huntington Gardens	80
In Praise of Trust, Old School	81
On My Way to J-Town	82
In Praise of the Irrational	84
Finding Rumi in Peru	87
Homebound Haiku	89
Winter Friend, the Pine	91
A Woman's Paper's Flying in the Wind	94
Release	97
In What Season Love, In What Season Dying	98
Notes	103
Acknowledgments	105

1

~ Small wisdom from a woman my age ~

Lee McCarthy

GUANYIN, GODDESS OF MERCY

I get more superstitious with age.
Heed the warnings of mystics and crones.
Believe less in random misfortune.
There's a mother who can stuff the devil in a bottle.

Heed the warnings of mystics and crones.
Guanyin listens to the cries of the world.
There's a mother who can stuff the devil in a bottle.
How much can she do to protect her child.

Guanyin listens to the cries of the world.
She must grow a thousand arms.
How much can she do to protect her child.
Sometimes the noise is unbearable.

She must grow a thousand arms.
To reclaim one more heart to kindness.
Sometimes the noise is unbearable.
Whose hand reaches out in the dark.

ELDER SISTER

—maybe i should have wanted less
Lucille Clifton, "Climbing"

To be old like you
no apology
for what you commit
in our common yearning

To forgive myself
my mothers' teachings,
that longings too eager
be concealed from view

Now that I'm able
to call out my name
a lifetime gleaned
from such furious ache

To be woman and know
I can simply say it
desire, my desire
is what keeps me

Here, open
to something so big
it can't only be mine
this growl

Growing sure
so rooted inside
even now when my bones
turn brittle and thin

This flowering
eye that shines
out of the dark
how ravenous

This mouth which still sings
as the red-tailed hawk
burns, born of the ancient
belly of need

The ache much sweeter
so close now
the lure, my willing
surrender.

AMONG THE CONTAINERS

Let me begin with hands, even bony
ones like mine, the skin too thirsty,
my long piano fingers stretching
two notes beyond an octave—

      or these small, cupped palms,
with their tiny harvests of water dripping
through fingered seams, my infant son's fist
gripping my thumb, his eyes still unable
to see, bound by entire oceans, and a hidden
sea fed by my tears—

              an entire saga
of hands carrying cups of steaming tea,
glasses, tumblers, goblets and mugs,
sake sets with missing pieces saved
from a long-ago wedding, an icy pitcher
of pink lemonade.

Or start with the mouth opening wide
as I come up for air, swimming
in a kidney shaped pool
on those hot summer nights,
not the short gasps on the walk home
from school, thick valley smog
tightening the chest, inhaling
quick and hard—

        the same mouth with its thin
upper lip, too many words trapped inside,
mouth with the too eager smile, nervous
with laughter, like giggling geishas
brimming with secrets, waiting so long
to savor one bite of satsuma plum.

Then this upstairs study, crammed
with letters and cards and a shrinking
memory which would all but vanish—

   if not for the 28 diaries,
the vacation and baby albums labeled
by season and year, stacks of unfinished
drafts and the thin manila folder
storing a no-nonsense surgical report—

   describing one 47-year-old
"gravida 1, para 1 Asian female with a right
adrenal mass," whose uterus and ovaries
are deemed medically expendable,
the moist, swollen lips of my sex now
wed to a riverless mouth—

   while the skinny
Lucille Clifton poem waits to be glued
in my scrapbook, its 39 synonyms
for light, from "gleam" to "flicker"
to "reflection," the final word "clear"
somehow curled in my ear.

SHAMISEN AND STRAW

—haiku based on photos from
Rural Japan: Radiance of the Ordinary

Tsunami

Snow on blue roof tiles—
sleeping village
      awakened by waves

The Way

Two strangers stop
on the road—wordless
      and bowing

In the Attic

Grandmother's shamisen—
who hears the plucking
      a heart brings

On a Samurai Scabbard

From silk and leather
wedding beauty and war—
      intricate knot

A Farmer Turns 80

Ragged straw hat
match the lines on his face—
      a hard-earned smile

Harvest Dreaming

After so much rain—
new rice seedlings
       remain hidden

Old Woman

Legs still strong enough
to dance—
       unexpected spring

THE BASKET

—Every object has its own breath.
  Museum of Indian Arts and Culture,
  Santa Fe, New Mexico

From each thin reed
so many small breaths

to know how much
can arise from seed

the minute inhalations
fed by groundwater and light

this stem that can bend
in the Southwest wind

~ ~ ~

A woman's story
that's braided

to grass, her
tireless hands

a noiseless weaving
one through another

slender fibers held
in endless thrum

~ ~ ~

Yellow moon and
her sisters

row upon row
intricate lacing

in measured
refrain, the long-

fingered memory
each basket saves

COMFORT WOMEN
—after reading about Yong Soo Lee, 87, testifying
in San Francisco, 2015

She was just fourteen
      says that fifteen men a day
           felt more like fifty

~ ~ ~

Translates to *ianfu*
      euphemism for *shofu*
           meaning—prostitutes

~ ~ ~

Even the doctor
      checking her for diseases
           makes sure he rapes her

~ ~ ~

Tricked, taken by force—
      will Japan apologize,
           the true story told?

~ ~ ~

She's eighty-seven
      sleeps three hours at a time
           may never forgive

~ ~ ~

Wrists tied with wire
        pain she couldn't imagine
                electric torture

~ ~ ~

Seventy years pass—
        the flashbacks and nightmares
                that won't let her out

NONE OF THESE WOMEN ARE SMILING

(Postcards from Mexico)

: Two Senoras at the Party

You will not see them on the dance floor,
not notice the newly permed hair,
the yellow and green dresses
with lace collars and hems,
not even the unblinking eyes.

You'll remember nothing about them
but the glitter and blur
of their red and silver shoes
which couldn't stop tapping
the whole night long.

: Keeping Vigil

Though these women of Oaxaca
still carry the bright red banners
of their men gone to battle,
their eyes have emptied—
fixed now on some place so far inside themselves
that an army of crows flies just overhead
and they never look up to the sky.

: Heading Home

She moves so quietly
through the cemetery
that she startles
the flock of starlings
resting there—

Within these white walls
beneath a cloudy
morning sky,
the flutter of one
hundred tiny wings.

SISTER MUSE

Just outside my window I see something white move across the pond.
Is it a fish? The thrust of a bird's pale wing. Then it's gone. I don't
believe in ghosts—and angels, at best, are human bound. A meteorologist
might tell me it's only a cloud reflected on the pond's surface. But right
now, in this New England forest, so far away from everything I know,
I could believe anything in this sacred place—burial ground for trees,
birds, deer, talking tribes who don't need words. Besides the familiar
maple, aspen, and pine, there are hazel, sassafras, sarsaparilla, even
four kinds of birch. After many generations, Pequot still inhabit the land.
So do descendants of Pilgrims and later generations of slaves brought
north. I'm only here for a few days, a visitor unfamiliar with this autumn
paradise, trying to ponder long held questions—here, where all the things
I call "my life" turn quiet and small in the midst of so much beauty,
the green trees revealing scattered branches of ripening yellows, reds,
and shades of orange impossible to name— all these colors mirrored
in the water. Keeping my eye on the pond, I watch a sudden ripple
of wind, causing the same wing-like motion I saw before. Then
the water shimmers, wind and light playing tricks with my mind,
as if a hermit fish rises up from the depths, or a sister muse submerged
far below, now drawn to these same brilliant hues, cannot help
but burst through.

IT ISN'T COINCIDENCE

Am I the only one
who sees the number 108
everywhere these days? At the tribal casino,
a penny slot machine with Chinese dragons
where I can bet 108 cents. Or last month's
World Series, where it took the Chicago Cubs
108 years to win again.
Like any good researcher, I've Googled
to learn it's not only auspicious, but divine,
in many religions. Buddhists and Taoists
hold malas with 108 prayer beads.
Hindus have 108 deities, even 108 energy
lines uniting to form the heart chakra.
In astronomy, the sun's diameter is about
108 times the earth's. And in nature,
math, and art, it's used in the formula
for the golden ratio—so pleasing,
whether in Da Vinci's Mona Lisa or
spiraling seashells and pinecones.
My husband thinks I'm too superstitious,
but I was born on the eighteenth
(18 x 6 = 108), and my 90-year-old
mother, who's one of the luckiest women
I know, just moved into
a retirement home, her apartment unit,
a perfect #108.

AN AFTERNOON WITH GUITAR SHORTY

What is it about the twang
of a blues guitar
that makes a woman like me
dance like she's twenty

Of a blues guitar
cry out and moan
dance like she's twenty
all pulse and hips

Cry out and moan
release this broken heart
all pulse and hips, this
boldness born from age

Release this broken heart
what is it about the twang
this boldness born from age
that makes a woman like me

ZUMBA GOLD AT 9 AM

We are a throng of older women—yes, we are silver and white-haired, or in my case, color-enhanced reddish brown, some with new knees & hips, others sporting flashy neon wristbands to tally how many steps, all of us ready to rumble in our rubber-soled shoes. Our teacher Yvonne used to weigh 300 pounds. Now, she zumbas & runs, sports a modified mohawk, sparkly bracelets stacked from wrist to forearm, & pink, lime, or lavender tank tops & sweats. Her constant command: "Smile! This is spoze to be fun!" And it is, though a few in the crowd just don't get the steps, their faces so labored & lost. Most of us, though, are having the best time we've had in decades, feel like we did in our teens, maybe better, since we no longer care if we look uncool—heck, no pressure anymore from ogling adolescents or lascivious men. Now, nothing matters more than the way this Latin music pulls us in—our bodies set loose to congas & timbales. We learn salsa, very New York City smooth, while Dominican merengue is frenzied & almost too fast to keep on beat. We all like the song where we gyrate our hips, follow Yvonne in an unhurried blend of hula & belly dance, then raise arms & hands to shoo away something toward the sky, all of us joining the chorus, "amor—amor, amor, amor," not sure if we're sending love out to the universe or saying goodbye to a lover, our voices rising as one. But my favorite, as always, is cha cha, which we got from Cuba. I didn't know this in the sixties when I cha cha cha'ed to Chicano & Motown discs, doing it Eastside-style with a swivel & dip. Cha cha feels like I'm coming home, so easy & free, just a zumba-crazed grandma with bad knees—that's me.

& MY FIVE DESIRES
—after Sesshu Foster's question

i.

riding a long, long breath
in a B-flat minor saxophone riff
to know the full arc of that unexpected
song where every single note
belongs

ii.

another bowl of pozole
with chopped avocado & tequila chasers
in sizzlin' Zihuatanejo

shops abuzz
in Espanol, Aztec trinkets,
Zapata t-shirts to bring back home

iii.

my own Einstein light bulb—
or at least a friendly
neighborhood mechanic
to navigate the how-and-why
of my cell phone or cable T.V.—
all voodoo in my ever humbling
electricians-and-geeks-are-like-gods
capitulation

iv.

cartilage for these broken knees
a new meniscus or patella
so I can kneel on the ground
to play with a grandson
pull weeds from the garden
scour my bathroom tiles

v.

just one more desire,
for just in case—
gourmet or folksy
as long as it's 100%
like real butter, leaded gasoline—
sweaty, earthy pungent,
even slightly toxic

one last tickle, grab & hook
for an aging girl like me

THIS HAND

whose 61-year-old veins
look like giant roots
breaking through earth's skin.

This hand I've filled
with stones
I find by the sea.

This hand fleshing
out a pine tree
with words or a brush,

waiting to be
thrilled one last time
before it empties.

ANCESTRAL SENTRIES

And yes—this is all about stones
        "sekimori-ishi" or boundary-guard stone—
used in Japanese gardens
        to guide visitors to the tea house—
the stone wrapped like a gift
        with rope or twine
                then knotted at the top.

It's also called "tome-ishi"
        or stop stone—a quiet way
to say the path is closed
        and yet, an invitation to find
the way in, an unspoken
        challenge to enter
                that place of wakening.

And if nothing more, I can honor
        this tradition by celebrating
the chosen rock and the rope
        encircling it—to reconnect the silent
part of me bound
        to the wordlessness
                of stone.

THE OLDER,
THE MORE

>—*ishigokoro*: the 'heart' or 'mind' of the rock

>—*Years, months, days, and hours are nothing but the mind.*
>   Dogen, 13th century Japan

. . . .

lately I feel I belong
to a mind so big—

                many calling it sacred
                others, love
                or breath

or love and breath and their unending need
        to go on

. . . .

the more I spend time with trees
or stones the more

        I'm certain

of tree mind, stone mind
        complex as my own

. . . .

take a tree, for instance
like the desert willow

                        I just planted

surely it knows

                        the violent upheaval
                        from one pot to the next

surely it carries

                        the centuries its ancestors
                        flourished in distant soil

look, three new buds

                        about to explode

part pink, part purple

                        so surely attentive

. . . .

some days I am struck
with the half-open

                        fragments
                        my world
                        moored in paradox

and yet
so many cues

                        whether a small perfect pebble
                        catching my eye

or that small truth
I stumble on, promise

                        not to forget

        our connections

. . . .

is this one encompassing mind
or is our starlit galaxy
                    to be found

in the incomparable particulars

my brief seven decades
                    dizzying
                  while still deliberate

and unexpected

                  pine trees
                  black stones
                  white rice

new poems

. . . .

the sky makes it obvious
just follow the clouds

                              infinite mind
                              shifting

between turbulence, calm

no wonder I watch
                              so closely
                              now

and feel so at home

2

*~ like the rusted wire
of a twisted and remembered fence ~*

Lawson Inada

36 VIEWS OF MANZANAR

> —among those taken away, my father's family
> the Francis M. Uyematsus of Montebello

1

How can a name be
so lovely but cruel:
Manzanar, the Spanish word
for apple orchard.

2

Manzanar, the first to open—
March of '42, Roosevelt
even uses the term
concentration camp, soon
replacing it with
the "more acceptable"
WRA relocation centers.

3

Camp equation:

540 acres + 8 guard towers + 36 blocks = 10,046 prisoners

4

Summer days over 110, winters below freezing
and that unending wind
drowning prisoners in dust and sand.

5

How often life depends
on political connections—
even in camp— my father
knows Paul Bannai,
a nisei buddy
with an early camp job.

Dad wrangles a deal
where the Uyematsus
originally assigned
to Heart Mountain
go to Manzanar instead.

Grandpa must donate
cherry trees in exchange
for moving to a camp
in California, not Wyoming,
less than 5 hours' drive
from Grandpa's nurseries.

6

Aunt Mare, now 92, the only
surviving Uyematsu internee

recalls being 15 and driven
to Manzanar in a government car.

There were 36 blocks and
first, the family lives in block 36

then re-assigned to 6-10-2
block 6 building 10 apartment 2

close to the laundry room
and the women's latrine.

7

Tar paper-covered barracks
with holes and slits
in the walls and doors—

Aunt Mare remembers
dirt piling up in the windows
and having to go outside
to shake sand out
from the bedding.

8

The next time you reach for
a Dr. Seuss book,
remember that Theodor Seuss Geisel
depicted Japanese as monster hordes

one cartoon shows "Jap Alley"
with Uncle Sam being attacked
by a mob of slant-eyed cats
carrying the imperial flag.

9

My own Uncle Sam,
only 9 years old in Manzanar,
remembers the tiny
rooms for families
and toilets squeezed together
with no stalls or partitions—

is Grandma one of the women
who make late-night trips
to the latrine for privacy
or who travels in pairs
holding up coats
as makeshift doors.

10

Many internees work
in camp, including Dad
who, early on, gets to pick
from a list just because
he's Paul Bannai's pal.

Dad's task: go through
stacks of books dropped off
by Army trucks as camp
gets ready to open school
and a library.

He's paid 12 bucks per month
and with three others
organizes the books—
describing it as
an "easy job."

11

Mess hall meals
are just that—a mess—

long lines
long tables
lousy food

parental authority
gone as kids run wild
teens escape boredom.

12

Only natural that the issei,
who excel as farmers,
nurserymen, flower growers,
will soon figure out

how to grow produce
design gardens and ponds
genius at coaxing green
from this dry desert soil

they even have contests
for the most beautiful
barracks garden—
the first winner, Block 34.

13

The Tomita boys crawl
under the barbed wire fencing
to go fishing at George Creek
with poles made from willow
and paper clip hooks
to catch rainbow trout.

So do others, as many as 400,
slipping out of camp for a day
or as long as two weeks—

Part of the challenge
to escape the armed guards
posted at watchtowers—
fresh trout and
temporary freedom
the delicious rewards.

14

Dad doesn't talk much about Manzanar
obtains a permit as soon as he can
to work farms in Utah and Idaho
harvesting sugar beets and potatoes

but he tells me about Aunt Alice
who's never able to enjoy her teens
she comes down with TB and after
release from camp, never recovers.

15

Within six months of opening, protests
and what authorities claim as a "riot,"
guards shooting into a crowd of 500.

James Ito from Los Angeles, only 17,
the first camp casualty—shot
through the abdomen and heart—his

mother dressed in the vest
James wears when he's killed,
a vest with a hole in the back.

16

Toyo Miyatake, already a well known
photographer before the war,
manages to smuggle a camera lens
and film plate holder into Manzanar.

At first taking pictures in secret, he
believes it's his duty to record camp life—
eventually Toyo is allowed
to be "official" camp photographer.

In one well-known shot, three boys
look out through the barbed wire,
in another, he poses his son holding
a pair of clippers against the fence.

17

There is even a monthly
newspaper in English—
everything from birth
and death announcements
to camp baseball team scores
and ads for Sears Roebuck—

dark humor in its title,
the *Manzanar Free Press*.

18

Remember who profit most
from putting Japanese behind barbed wire:
the Hearst corporation,
white farmers who want the acres
our issei have transformed
into fertile farmland,
neighbors who loot households
vacated during the camp years,
businessmen like Manchester Boddy
who buys Grandpa's total inventory,
over 300,000 camellias,
far below what they're worth—
or as Dad puts it, Boddy plunders
Grandpa's plants "for a song."

19

Not even a full year
when internees
must answer
a loyalty questionnaire—

A "yes" on #27 means
you're willing
to fight in
U.S. armed forces

A "yes" on #28 means
you swear unqualified
allegiance to the country
that's locked you up

One Manzanar internee's
response: "What
do they know
about loyalty?"

20

July 27, 1942 front page
from the *Manzanar Free Press*:
"Mrs. Karl Yoneda, 4-2-2-,
who, singlehanded, produced
four nets per day"
breaking a record
at the camouflage factory.

21

In high school Aunt Mare joins
a girls' club—the Wee Funsters
that parties with handsome guys
who belong to the Manza-Knights,

she remembers Ralph Lazo—
doesn't find out till camp is over
Ralph isn't Japanese but chooses
to join his nisei high school friends.

22

By September of '42
only 26 of the 57
white teachers hired
to work at Manzanar
show up—

the qualified evacuees
used as aides
to fill in the gap
earn $16 a month,
teachers, $135.

23

Tatsuo Kunitomi, aged 12, asks
his sister— "What's the use
of studying American history
when we're behind barbed wire?"

24

Only 14, Hank Umemoto looks out
his barrack window—a majestic Mt. Whitney
against an indigo sky—vowing
one day to climb to the top.

He never forgets his promise—
reaching the mountain summit,
over 14,000 feet high,
at the unlikely age of 71.

25

Baseball, basketball, and more
for both kids and adults
Team names like the Yahoodies,
Manza-Bombers, Aloha Ramblers

Monikers like "Puk" and "Boots"
and "Pardon My Looks"

Sports already common in J-A life
even more essential in prison camp.

26

At Mom's retirement home
I interview Frank Kikuchi—
a nisei deejay at Manzanar.

Smiling, Frank recounts how
he and buddy Archie Miyatake
played those 40s big band hits—

Jimmy Dorsey, Glenn Miller—
so kids can jitterbug
and slow dance.

Refreshments include
Kool-Aid punch
and egg salad sandwiches.

27

August is the month of obon—
a Buddhist festival to honor
the ancestral spirits—

Even at Manzanar in 1942
and by the next year
thousands turning out

To watch 1600 dancers
clad in colorful kimonos
join the bon odori circle.

28

Grandpa trucks in cherry trees
from his Montebello nursery

for a garden constructed
outside the Children's Village.

Manzanar's orphanage includes
kids from white foster families,

infants as young as 6 months,
children from Alaska to San Diego.

Army Col. Bendetsen says, "if they
have one drop of Japanese blood."

For many of the 101 wards
camp is the first family they know.

At war's end many have
no guardian to claim them

and Grandpa never finds out
where his cherry trees end up.

29

Just six miles north,
the town closest
to Manzanar
is named Independence.

30

24 years later
the first annual
Manzanar pilgrimage—

nisei survivors
sansei activists
paying homage—

a tradition
carried on
since 1969.

31

An interfaith obelisk
is built in the cemetery
to honor the deceased—
Buddhists and Christians together,
every family donating
ten to fifteen cents each
to purchase concrete—

"Ireito" inscribed
in black kanji characters,
"soul consoling tower"
their literal translation—
the white stone monument
still stands after
seventy-seven years.

32

In 1992 Manzanar is named
a national historic site—
exactly 50 years after FDR
signs the executive order
rounding up 120,000
innocent Japanese Americans.

Visitors can now walk through
reconstructed barracks,
younger generations locating
our grandparents' names
from the thousands listed
in alphabetical order.

33

Questions I wish
I could ask
my issei grandparents

Francis and Kuniko
who don't speak English,
who don't live long enough
to hear the President's apology:

Grandpa, did you find
comfort tending to your
cherry trees, watering
your wisteria—
and Grandma, did you keep
writing tanka, your feelings
about camp?

34

Scores of books
from history to memoir:
Farewell to Manzanar
in the high school
curriculum where I teach—

But still, too many voices
unheard, too many stories
that will never be told.

35

The collective chant
at Manzanar pilgrimages:
"Don't Repeat History."

After 9/11, pilgrimages
include Muslims
who've become targets.

Recent calls grow even louder
as migrant families are separated,
children imprisoned in border jails.

36

When my Uncle Sam turns 70,
we talk about driving
to Manzanar together
to visit the camp after
so many decades—

he dies before
we ever get the chance.

THE BACHI-BACHI
BUDDHAHEAD BLUES

Even over-Americanized sansei like me
know about *bachi*,
that Japanese karma warning:
if misfortune strikes,
it's payback for wrongs
we did, or maybe crimes
by some reckless ancestor.

Examples of possible *bachi*
seen everywhere. A kid playing
a prank on his brother, and
the next day a pigeon poops
on his head. A coach, who's too
harsh with her team, losing her
voice at the title match.

But can this blame game
explain every misfortune? Does
bachi explain why I got breast cancer
my first year retired? Too twisted
and cruel, a Pearl Harbor *bachi*
forcing 120,000 of us into
barbed wire camps.

Most JA's save
bachi I-told-you-so's
for less extreme events,
wondering which
of the thousand dumb things
we do today will come back
to haunt and roost.

Way back when in the old country,
bachi was a handy tool to keep
spoiled children and wandering
husbands in line. And now,
generations later, aging sansei
who hear bad news often chime
in unison, "*Bachi.*"

Little Tokyo hardly resembles
the J-town I visited with Grandma,
but *bachi* feels ingrained—
"*Summer of the Big Bachi,*"
a popular sansei book title,
and a *Bachi Burger* joint
just down the block.

SO ARE WE BECOMING MORE VISIBLE
—January, 2019

Say what?—a Korean woman co-hosting
last week's Golden Globes before a main
floor table of gorgeous and formerly ignored
actresses from "Crazy Rich Asians."

Anyone under 20 knows about K-pop's
BTS, pretty-boy band to-the-max, bringing
a uniquely South Korean pop/hip-hop sound
to screaming girls at New York's Citi Field.

Or Steve Aoki, coolest DJ who's not only
Japanese American and over 40,
but can still rock dance floors and stadiums
as he jumps non-stop with adoring fans.

Now I'm J-A too and could argue
we've always been visible—
120,000 of us getting locked up
in World War II concentration camps.

But that was 7 decades ago
and in the meantime, we were pretty
much invisible and blocked from
the film and music scene.

Asian actors from America
were mostly ignored—
"Sulu" George Takei and
Bruce Lee, notable exceptions.

When I was twenty, I found refuge
in the little-known Toho La Brea Theater,
a sansei swooning over Toshiro Mifune,
yearning to see an all-Asian cast

While Hollywood still perpetuates
what we've experienced all our lives—
getting asked where we come from,
mixed up in one "Oriental" stew.

Aging baby-boomers like me still
demand yellow power for American-born
actors, uncertain about our seeming
growing presence on screen.

Today, I can find Asian faces like mine
on primetime TV, from Korean soaps
to "Fresh Off the Boat" to fellow sansei
Carrie Inaba on "Dancing with the Stars."

Who can say how much social media
has made things easier,
Psy's "Gangnam Style" getting
one billion views on YouTube—

Or on Facebook, I just saw The Hu Band's
bad-ass motorcycle-riding Mongolians
playing horsehead fiddle and tovshuur guitar
throat singing about Genghis Khan.

Any given night, I can spot at least one
to many nameless Asian Americans
in TV ads, perhaps the ultimate dollar-flashing
sign of our newfound screen visibility

And who knew that TV coverage
of figure skating would be crowded
with record-breaking jumpers like Nathan Chen
or youngster newcomer Alysa Liu

But call me stuck in the 60s, I always
cheer loudest for our own homegrown
stars—from James Shigeta to Mako,
Anna May Wong, Margaret Cho

and no band comes close to the inimitable
sansei soul of LA's Hiroshima, blending
koto with electric keyboard, taiko with sax,
our feet gratefully tapping to a *J-Town Beat*.

PANDEMIC POSTSCRIPT: OR ARE WE TOO VISIBLE AGAIN
—April, 2020

This season Asian Americans are the targets—
        the president pointing his finger at China
but no difference if we're Chinese or Korean,
Japanese, Pilipino, Vietnamese, Hmong—

        Because in a country ingrained
in white privilege, slavery, genocide
we get the dubious and ever-changing
        honor of being invisible, a model minority,

Or "Yellow Peril" scapegoats—
"It's your fault!" "Go back to China!"
        Calling Covid-19 the Chinese virus
is enough to incite the mob.

We are warning each other
to take extra precautions
when riding the subway
        or going to the market—

Don't be surprised if a non-Asian
curses, pushes you, spits in your face—
        one woman taking her trash out
is doused and burned with acid.

Actor John Cho reminds us:
we belong here "conditionally,"
the masks worn for this pandemic
        not nearly enough to protect us.

I WISH I'D SEEN MY NISEI FATHER DANCE

Before the war nisei were so much cooler
than we sansei kids give them credit—
after all they could listen to Meiji-farmer folk songs
and siblings practicing violin and shamisen
while finger snapping to Glenn Miller, Benny Goodman,
and Old Blue Eyes on the radio.

>Dad swears the girls were prettier in his day—
>he drove a tan convertible, thanks to a father
>who got rich selling flowers in the 30s,
>with extra pocket money that got him
>into trouble with poorer yogore,
>his Boyle Heights friends protecting him.

I've been told my father was popular
among the girls—not for his looks,
but because he could really dance:
the swing, fox trot, a mean jitterbug.
Was he ever called a "jive-bomber"
or "cloud-walker" for his nimble feet?

>Dad was going to school in Chicago
>when Japan bombed Pearl Harbor
>and within 24 hours, the FBI
>was escorting him
>from the college dormitory
>to a train back to California.

Lucky for him, he didn't stay long
in Manzanar with his family.
He worked potato farms in Idaho,
got into college in Lincoln, Nebraska,
met my 19-year-old Mom, prettier
than any girl he'd ever danced with.

                And after the war, nothing could
                stop the nisei from still having their dances—
                not new babies and bills, neighborhoods
                that wouldn't let them move in. I've seen
                the photos, Dad and Mom all decked out
                in wide lapel suit and full skirted dress.

THE SUITCASE
—a Manzanar tale

In 1945 Dad and Grandpa
get a travel permit from Manzanar
officials to visit Star Nurseries,
the business Grandpa starts
back in the '30s and flourishes
even in the Depression years.
They take a bus bound for L.A.

Stopping in the small town
of Mojave, Dad tells
Grandpa to stay on the bus—
knowing the war is still
being fought, and how
dangerous it is for them—
but Grandpa gets off anyway.

Like many issei, Grandpa
is short—5'2" at the most—
not exactly threatening,
but as he walks downtown
the cops arrest him, put
Grandpa and Dad in jail
to spend the night.

Around 2 AM, FBI agents
pick them up and drive
them to Fresno, never
suspecting the hatchet
Grandpa packs in his suitcase,
the hatchet not so unusual for
this gifted plant grower.

Dad recalls how dark it is
on the winding mountain roads.
Already nervous, he starts to panic
when one of the agents turns on
the light inside the car, looks
hard at both of them
sitting in the back seat.

Dad warns Grandpa, speaking
in Japanese, "Don't do anything
to make them suspicious."
The FBI never inspects the suitcase.
Once in Fresno, they are questioned
then put back on a bus to L.A.—
Grandpa's hatchet in tow.

LITTLE TOKYO HAIKU, 2019

I want to go back—
        this hip, touristy J-town
                would make Grandpa cry

While we were in camp
        the streets jumped to Bronzeville jazz,
                and then we returned

Just twenty-five bucks,
        a train ticket, camp to home—
                Mom cannot forget

San Kwo Low is gone—
        so is the best almond duck
                I ever tasted

It's *chinameshi*,
        Chinese food made J-A style,
                affordable too

Sidewalks filled with foodies,
        sansei with hapa grandkids
                and all these homeless

Skateboards and pink hair,
        more common in J-town than
                issei descendants

Old as my Grandpa,
        I keep looking for faces
                resembling my own

LOVE-IN FOR JEREMY LIN

It's a win-win-win and I'm all in
for Mr. Jeremy Lin.

No one could imagine an Asian American
NBA sensation in this year of the dragon

It's a win-win-win, yes, I'm all in
for Mr. Jeremy Lin.

And how can I begin, it's not just about skin
though I feel we're like kin as I watch this kid spin

with his kinda silly grin. Unaccustomed to the din
he's a real genuine, plus he's smart within,

to Harvard he has been
and he can take it on the chin

It's a win-win-win, are you all in
for Mr. Jeremy Lin?

HOW TO BECOME A BETTER NOODLE POET

Choose your noodle carefully.

Let's focus today on ramen.
Other days we might groove
to curry laksa or saimin,
to guksu, bean threads, or pho.

For our noodle of choice,
immerse it in a delectable brew:
fish-based, pork-soaked,
clear veggie broths.

Garnish with handfuls
of finely chopped scallions.

Build layers of tastiness,
from surface to secret interiors
add your own particulars:
pink fish cake, garden greens,
a perfectly poached egg yolk.

A memorable bowl of steaming
noodles can tantalize all five senses,
including the ears as we listen
for our boisterous slurping.

Know that no two noodle-istas
compose the same song—no
your noodle is better than mine
in this poet's kitchen.

Learn to make every bite float
on the tongue, then dive.

DEAR LAWSON

>—after seeing "I Told You So," Alan Kondo's 1974 film
>on poet Lawson Inada

Did you know you were the very first
poet I ever heard? Round about 1970—
UCLA, early guest speaker in
Asian American Studies—you
were one of us—angry, young, militant—
and yet you weren't. You "talked the talk"
but only like a poet who plays upright bass
and loves straight ahead jazz. Man,
you sure knew how to riff.

With a bebop ear, you
embraced "yellow power" too—
ranting about the "E.H.W."—
Eternal Honkies of the World—
or proclaiming:
>*Wake up—we are king*
>*kong over this world*
and
>*sing! Think Yellow!*

You even gave us homework—
write poems using loaded words
like "media," "Asian," "identity."
I went home and did just that—
been writing poems ever since.

The first poetry book I bought
was *Before the War*—for just five bucks.
Its dust jacket, torn from so much use,
pictured you in black-and-white on the back—
serious, wearing your signature beret

as you sit in front of a sign demanding
"Fresno Needs a Progressive Leader."
Still in my early twenties, I had a major crush
on Toshiro Mifune—but Lawson, you
were the hero that changed me.

Just last month I saw you for the first time
on film in "I Told You So." Hope you don't mind
my saying there's a bit of a gangsta strut
as you walk the sidewalks of downtown Fresno.
Cool as ever in your turtle neck, wool cap,
slightly flared denims, looking at old Westside
signs—"Nisei Barber Shop," "Azteca,"
"El Gato Negro Cafe"—walls filled with
neighborhood graffiti and Chicano murals—
singing,
    I told you so, oh yes . . . I told you so, oh yes.

Your poems salute so many jazz greats—
like Mingus, Coltrane, Parker, Monk.
You even got Billie Holiday's autograph
when you were eighteen and tell us
it was around that time you began
writing poetry—

    Then start the music playing—
    thick jazz, strong jazz—

        and notice that the figure
    comes to life:

sweating, growling
over an imaginary bass—

My friend Taiji, who also plays
bass, says he hears jazz whenever
you perform.

But what the name Lawson Inada
means most to me is all
you've written about the concentration camps
and our history as Japanese Americans.
Just a sansei kid in Rowher and Amache,
you depict camp imprisonment
with wisdom and outrage, unblinking
and undeniable truths:

> *Mud in the barracks—*
> *a muddy room, a chamber pot.*
>
> *Mud in the moats*
> *around each barracks group.*
>
> *Mud on the shoes*
> *trudging to the mess hall.*

And I suspect you're addressing
a lot of us "movement" sansei
when you write:

> *People ask: "Why didn't you protest?"*
> *Well, you might say: "They had **hostages**."*

You so rightly attest—

> *And the people*
> *made poetry*
> ***from*** *camp.*

> *And the people*
> *made poetry*
> ***in*** *camp.*

Yes, "the people made poetry"—
our determination to create beauty
in defiance of barbed wire jails,
so much art and artifacts made with hands
and hearts—the bonsai gardens, wood carvings,
sketches and paintings, furniture, tankas,
jewelry—using whatever we could find.

> *I told you so, oh yes . . . I told you so*

Thank you, Lawson, for celebrating
men like Yosh Kuromiya,
Heart Mountain draft resistor—

> *Arrested, judged,*
> *sentenced, imprisoned*
> *. . .*
> *for refusing*
> *induction*

Back in the day, do you remember
a lot of us carried Mao's "little red book,"
espoused the idea of art "for the people."
Well, your poetry comes from exactly that place—
our issei and nisei roots, the camps, a uniquely
American story of struggle and resistance.
No wonder so many of us have grown
from your words.

And as we used to sign off, Lawson—
All power.

SISTER STONE

i

These are the stones that sing to me
not the granite boulders
        transported from canyons
or rocks the size for hurling
        like those thrown at Grandpa
                when he came to America

The stones I choose are washed in by the tides
their ocean sleek skins
        polished by current and time
the sheen of wet black
        on these pebbles I save
                like treasure

ii

A wise man says, "The stones cry out,"
and even the most ordinary rock
        carries a history
rapturous as the stars
        bursting sky and mountain
                with longing

iii

My early ancestors built gardens of gravel
the dry landscape a place
       for meditation
our monks tending to
       seas of white stones
              with rakes

At Manzanar issei and nisei inmates
searched the Sierra bajadas
       for bedrock
to create barrack gardens
       camp ponds and parks
              for solace

And I have long called myself
a stone lover
       somehow knowing
my unfinished story is also carried
       in the wordless stones
              that fill my path

3

~ into the sharp edge of seasons ~

Lucille Clifton

~ my human voice heard its blue voice ~

Linda Hogan

THIS TREE, THAT TREE

One poet reveals
a god sheltered
in every tree

Another claims
the young girl
who spirits a tree

Maybe it's truth
roots reaching roots
far beneath feet

Maybe it's age
retelling forest folklore
trunk to limbs to sky

Or simply a promise
of sakura blossoms
unfolding each spring

WHEN THE WORLD AGREES ON NOTHING

Even the Chinese elms
that line my walk at dusk become
a weary long-armed tribe
whose ragged branches crowd
the twilight sky,
their limbs in disarray.

Inside this corridor
there's an oddly comforting
sense of chaos, the noise
of a car rushing by
can't penetrate the stillness.

Before the last light dissolves,
dozens of invisible birds burst out
like dark, silent buds
from trunks and upper branches
to flee into a starless night.

I recall a little girl playing with
her sister, their arms outstretched,
as I witness this outbreak
of voiceless birds
in a sky so brittle that
all the trees
contort in greeting.

WINTER, 2016

> —*Winter in America*
> *And ain't nobody fighting*
> *'Cause nobody knows what to save*
>   from "Winter in America," Gil Scott-Heron, 1974

There's fresh blood on the sidewalk
    and everyone's afraid to touch it.

No street or bed is safe.
    My throat is parched and no amount

of water soothes it. I don't
    recognize the sound of my own voice—

I'm sure I've been screaming
    in my sleep. Did I ask about the body

carried away in the night? Did I
    do anything different, knowing we can't love

our lives in the old way.
    I'm not sure what to pray for anymore,

not sure how to drum back
    the dread in this unrecognizable heart,

to quiet the unceasing drone
    of America's long winter rain.

THE PANTHERS

President's Day weekend, 2018—"Black Panther,"
    the new Marvel comic film, breaking records
        for ticket sales. Many young fans, too young to know
about the Black Panthers of my generation. It's the same

Feeling of ethnic pride as fifty years ago, when
    Oakland Black Panthers served free breakfasts to children,
        two '68 Olympics medal winners gave the black power salute,
and we sang with James Brown, "I'm black and I'm proud,"

Even if we weren't black. Revolutionary change—the new normal then,
    let it remain the new normal now—with "Black Lives Matter,"
        NFL players on bended knee, women's marches from coast
to coast, high school students demanding anti-gun laws.

Fifty years ago, when Martin was killed, who could imagine
    we'd elect Barack Obama just four decades later,
        hip hop music and dance would be global staples,
Claudine Rankine's *Citizen*, the only poetry bestseller.

Superheroes are nothing new in the struggle, only this time
    a Disney movie is giving every boy and girl, young and old,
        that big screen sensation of fighting for justice—
as normal as Rosa Parks, Malcolm X, Harriet Tubman, on and on.

Let us bridge the generations and remind all who will listen
    that it only takes one woman sitting on a bus to inspire hundreds,
        one farmworker, one union activist, one parent
to build a movement based on the power of the people.

AMERICAN SUMMER: 8 TANKA

The hottest ever
  in country after country
ice caps keep melting
  rain forests shrinking
     —rising sea of denial

I may need to flee
  these hostile streets of LA
escape the road rage
  sidestep the homeless, heed
     —the slouching beast set free

The once lovely tweets
  of robins and nightingales
are no longer heard
  just non-stop babble
     —unique to humans with phones

Slaughter and plunder
  slavery and prison camps
ask any Native
  or dark-skinned victims
     —the price of not being white

When he says, "Go back,"
  does he mean where I was born?
California
  three generations
     —the only homeland I know

Baseball on TV
   now my favorite distraction
from the breaking news
   savor a few hours
       —return to waking nightmare

This wanna-be king
   tweeting all hours of the night
fires up his base
   with falsehoods and fear
       —laughs all the way to the bank

Prisons for profit
   brown babies torn from mothers
bullies with torches
   oligarchs and snakes
       —July, 2019

UNRELENTING THIS HEAT / UNFORGIVING THIS JULY

I want to write about clouds and stones / the pleasure they give me usually takes over / but not this time / my country of birth the only country I know the country I protested / where I witnessed true change / is this country I no longer know / the latest lie or despicable act / all we can talk about / the idea of we / distorted to your side or mine / and yet I am sure we remain connected / we are clouds and stones and mothers and birds / though I just saw a falcon in my garden / a tiny songbird in its dangerous beak / the victim about to be eaten / so easy the leap now / this dread of things falling apart / almost like watching us being eaten alive / though we are still here / uncertain onlookers to an unending litany / unthinkable crimes becoming ordinary truths / in this unfamiliar country where we are / the divided and the conquered / I hear more commotion in my backyard trees / birds crying out / even crashing the living room window / afraid the falcon will strike again / there's a screaming inside I can't soften or silence / I can't convince anyone / we are all connected / we are clouds and stones and worlds at war / no matter how broken / always connected / no matter how deadly / we are mothers and birds / so closely connected / we are

CHINESE SNOWBALLS AT HUNTINGTON GARDENS

—for Ellen and Bob

For a few hours our minds are happy captives
of plants and trees in full April bloom,
recent rains returning a truer green
to our LA landscape, even the cacti
grateful for the plentiful showers
which broke years of drought.

We forget the danger that fills our nightly
news, the warnings from journalists,
that feeling of being bombarded
from every direction with no escape—
yet we do, set free in these gardens
seeded from every continent.

Who would guess there are so many
types of aloe, both local and as faraway
as Madagascar and Brazil?
The Japanese maples are peaking
in bright red and crimson, while
Chinese snowball trees burst
with festive white pom-poms.

So much beauty, enough
for all who pay attention—whether
hummingbird or freeway driver,
honeybee, lizard, or goose—
the world raging outside impossible
to bring into this conversation.

IN PRAISE OF TRUST, OLD SCHOOL

As in the not too distant past—before instant bill pays and internet spying, when I could still put checks for my rent and car loan in that nearby corner mailbox, or answer the phone call from someone I actually know. It's almost Halloween, and we used to go house to house without our parents, no fear of kidnap, poisoned popcorn balls or razors hidden in apples. When did we start looking behind us no matter where we walk, even my own driveway? When did a social security number and date of birth become something I'd need to guard like gold, even my lousy tax returns liable to get stolen. Back in the 70s we were studying Marxism in clandestine study groups, afraid our lines had been tapped by good ole Uncle Sam (well, more like scary J. Edgar). Now it's pretty much accepted that privacy is gone, and marketers, the military, Amazon, and greedy hackers know everything about me—from the latest pair of sneakers I've bought to which candidate I'll vote for. It's already yesterday's news when banks, hospitals, retail chains, credit protection services are attacked. Normal for me to watch the cars in front and behind me, left side and right, to see if the driver is texting and likely to crash into mine. Being an older pedestrian used to mean drivers would stop for you and wave you through the crosswalk. Now I risk being run over even when the light turns green—the WALK sign telling me to move forward. Ain't trusting that anymore, too many cars that accelerate just to beat me as I step off the curb. And don't even mention post 9/11 flying! The endless lines, being x-rayed and patted down, having to fit my toiletries into those teeny 1-quart plastic bags. Oh, how I miss the twentieth century when I didn't have to constantly think of being ripped off or assaulted. Acts of random kindness have been taken over by acts of mean indifference and haphazard aggression. Who said your gratification or mine must be instant? What makes any impulse worthy of public broadcast, even reckless presidential tweets shaping foreign policy? I'm sure I don't speak for most of you, but I could—I really could—return to a time when we took trust for granted, our lives not yet governed by laptops and selfies and this lunatic oh-so-addictive SPEED!

ON MY WAY TO J-TOWN

: At San Pedro & Second

He walks toward me,
right down the center of this
crowded street, daring drivers
who swerve out of his way.
I am stopped at the signal.
He rushes toward me,
glaring hard as he removes
his wool cap to slap my hood.
He's homeless but unlike
the others, whose eyes
are dazed, he feels menacing.
Little Tokyo seems to be his turf,
and he's not the least bit happy
seeing another car with
a Japanese face like mine.

: Waiting to Cross Main

In his forties, or even fifties,
a homeless man who looks Asian—
perhaps from Laos or Cambodia—
in a city where most who wander
the streets are not Asian
and push shopping carts
almost too heavy to move.
But this man's arms are free—
over his heavy coat,
a long bunch of five or six
carefully enlaced plastic

bags dangle from each
shoulder—everything he needs
in this life just light
enough to carry.

: By City Hall

The light's turned green but
traffic has stopped. Who finally
emerges is a man on a bicycle,
slowly making his way across
First Street but going in circles.
Once he reaches the sidewalk,
he keeps riding in loops
while we all move on.
"Just another crazy" is what
many think but I can't
forget him, wonder about
all the wars we're fighting—
especially these latest assaults,
the undeniable dread
that's spreading within us—
as we try to go on
with our regular lives,
knowing the very idea of
normal has become
so distorted a man
biking in circles
and holding up traffic
makes perfect
and welcome sense.

IN PRAISE OF THE IRRATIONAL

: Kanpai (that's Japanese for "cheers")

Hooray for the illogical,
this tale of built-in contradictions,
each perilous paradox that can
drive us bananas—and the curious
ways we keep the faith.

There's a logic to zero—
ask any mathematician, poet or priest—
but don't expect them
to explain.

There's a profound dependability
in the irrational instincts
of women—yes us—all
tenderness, guts, and a fierceness
no man will ever fathom.

: Round and Round

Among the most famous
in the irrational numbers family—
pi, the empress of unending
and unrepeating digits—
secret to binding diameters
to perfect circles,
simplified for students
as $\pi = C / d$.

"How beautiful," says
a man who can recite
over 23,000 digits of pi—
recalls them by certain
colors and forms—
some, like 3-2-8, conjure
a mountain of lime and blue,
or 7-5-6, a bromeliad bloom.

If I asked you your favorite
earthly shape, you might say
a round ball at the age of seven
or that milk-scented areola
before you could talk.
Long ago we worshipped
suns and moons, laid out
stones in the shape of circles.

It was no small leap
to invent riding on wheels,
or capture life's crazy imbalance
with the yin/yang symbol—
even better the Zen circle
embracing all and nothing
in just one or two
strokes of the brush.

And maybe I'm in
on a secret I don't understand—
no accident that since last night's yoga

I'm now caught in the spell
of an ancient brass gong—
ripple after ripple, encircling
some tiny region
of my heart unbound.

FINDING RUMI IN PERU
—September, 2019

1

Before I met you, I'd keep returning to love poems by Neruda and Rumi.
For me, Neruda had an earthiness that made me feel skin and rain
and sweet summer corn. But Rumi took me to an unexplainable place,
weightless, radiant with delight and wonder.

And when we started to fall in love, though you were not a poet,
you were also familiar with Neruda and Rumi—I knew you were unlike
the other men I'd been with. It's said that when reciting his poems,
Rumi would turn round and round, some even called him the 'drunken
Sufi.' One night we found ourselves at a whirling dervish performance,
the Sufi dancers spinning and spinning like we were those first months
together—whirling ourselves into a world only we could know. And
even now, after all these years, when we dance we keep opening
some secret door into music, frenzy and surrender.

2

We've grown old but not too old to journey to Peru, Machu Picchu
our destination. In the Sacred Valley, we go to Ollantaytambo, an Inca
fortress built in the rocky hillside. Ollantaytambo, Patakancha, Urubamba—
names with a melodic rhythm that's new to me. We walk through
the cobble-stoned streets of the village and a store sign catches my eye:
"Rumi." Excited, I tell our guide how much I love Rumi. She does
not know the poet, explaining that rumi means stone in the ancient
Quechua language. My excitement grows—how perfect a connection—
so many of my poems contain rumi—from the tiny grey gravel in Zen

gardens to black pebbles I bring home from the beach, river sculptures made from balancing stones of every size and shape, the elegant boulder a nisei gardener trucks home from the local San Gabriels to anchor his Japanese garden. And now these massive granite stones the Incas used to build Machu Picchu, a palace high in the Andes six centuries ago. Fitting, that Machu Picchu means "old mountain."

3

Rumi, the poet.
Rumi, the stone.

HOMEBOUND HAIKU
—Spring, 2020

Unstoppable spring—
burst of green on bare branches
      virus without bounds

Which is scarier—
bullets, viral pandemics,
      a mob ruled by fear

No time to prepare—
a self-absorbed president's
      lies and excuses

Still taking our walks
we are struck by the orange
      of this season's poppies

The streets so quiet
no children at the playground
      but the bluest skies

Now that you stay home
I am cooking up a storm—
      our waistlines thicken

How to stay healthy—
Netflix, old books, new poems
      sustain that deep breath

No more zumba class—
so last night I shut my door
        cha-cha'ed my heart out

We need bigger masks
to hide our Asian faces—
        we're targets again

A two-month lockdown?
Grandpa confined at Gila
        three relentless years

I used to teach math
but it took a pandemic
        for graphs to take hold

These are the hard facts—
I'm older than 65
        may not make the cut

The cruelest spring—
we watch the rising death toll,
        cherry blossoms too

WINTER FRIEND, THE PINE

Even before I learned my name
contains "*matsu*," Japanese for pine tree,
it seemed to be part of my own
genetic destiny. Generations
of Uyematsus lived on Izu Peninsula,
home to cedar, cypress, and pine.
No one told me about an ancestral
reverence to matsu that would
have made much more sense
than the 50s Americana I was
raised on. LA's eucalyptus,
pepper and jacaranda trees fill
my girlhood memories, yet I'll
always gravitate to pine.

On a trip to King's Canyon,
when I am eight or nine,
alone with pine
trees overhead, the sound
of water rushing
nearby—and I feel
something bigger than
anything I've ever felt—
impossible to forget.

How comforting to learn,
so many years later,
that in Shinto legend,
gods and goddesses
descended on

pine tree branches,
their spirits still residing
inside. On matsu planted
at Shinto shrines, *omikuji*,
fortune-telling paper strips
holding both blessings
and curses, are tied to
the branches to ensure
good luck.

I've planted a kuro-matsu,
Japanese black pine,
in my front yard garden.
Surrounded by mossy
grass, it stands out
in my very urban
neighborhood, crowded
with houses and cars
and low maintenance
landscapes. A tiny treasure,
it may well be the most
gorgeous plant—a welcome
aberration—on this
ordinary cul-de-sac.

Recently I've discovered
the pine tree is central
to Noh play scenery
and in Heian poetry

it's linked with
waiting for a lover.
Clusters of paired
pine needles that drop
to the ground are
symbols of fidelity.
And in Japanese
shochikubai refers to
the three friends of winter—
pine, bamboo and plum.

While winter approaches
in so many different ways,
I continue to take in
the season's uncertainties
with endless little beauties—
—like today's microscopic
photos of pine stems,
in eye-boggling cross
sections of intricate
purples and blues,
or this latest handful
of pine needles, still
lovely and green
on my open palm.

A WOMAN'S PAPERS FLYING IN THE WIND

i

Seven travelers on foot
        hold onto their straw hats
                with these unexpected gusts.

One is a woman with arms extended,
        helpless while her papers
                scatter and float away—

As trees bend and leaves
        rip from branches, she won't forget
                a steadfast Mount Fuji.

ii

All of my ancestors came from Shizuoka,
        the prefecture south of Tokyo
                whose boundaries straddle
    the land where the volcanic Fuji
            erupted 100,000 years ago.

I probably know this beloved mountain best
        because of my love for woodblock prints,
            my favorite art form,
        never tiring of Hokusai's
            masterful "36 Views."

I will never know if my grandparents
        who emigrated to America
                in their twenties,
        ever climbed Fuji
                before leaving Japan.

But I do know Grandma Kuniko
        wrote poetry like many issei,
                sent tanka penned in kanji
        to the *Rafu* and *Kashu Mainichi*,
                bilingual press in LA.

Like those papers lost in the wind
        in Hokusai's woodblock,
                none of the poems
        my grandmother wrote
                were ever saved.

iii

I've been told I look like
        the grandma who wrote tanka,
                though she never learned
        English, never talked to her
                Americanized grandkids.

Would she be surprised
        that I'd one day turn
                to poetry, even reveal
        family stories she might want
                to keep secret.

Would I tell her I finally saw Mt. Fuji
        in person—the October sky so blue
                after dense morning fog,
        our guide saying again
                how lucky and rare.

RELEASE

—Let me work on memory, on thought, how to level the horizon . . .
Ray Gonzalez, *"Forth"*

Lately we do our foolhardy best to level the horizon—
      light jagging and slicing
           through everything we thought we knew.

Out of habit we blame the other, don't protect
      our most vulnerable,
           ride on the same tired words.

No matter how off balance, we try to mold memory
      into the shape of "before,"
           trapped in this endless ungrounding.

The scales of history tip furiously backwards
      as the orphan sky bleeds on through the night,
           these outstretched hands unanswered.

How long must we wait
      to see the horizon shift at least eighteen degrees,
           love in its most demanding proportions—

With death ever imminent, how to fulfill
      one more chance to become who we must be,
           to gratefully surrender.

IN WHAT SEASON LOVE,
IN WHAT SEASON DYING

summer festival

long after dream / a memory of rice fields / this August moon

whose wordless aching / ancestral spirits / flickering lights

on these crowded streets / taiko drumbeats / dancers who beckon

I'm old now too / join the circle of fools / long into night

silence teases

with her caw and chirp / bare rustle of leaf / invisible jet's hum

mind's whispered chatter / endless trickle / for sky's blue ear

inside a trembling / this honeysuckle bush / heavy with blossom

what rush of wings / all flutter and swoop / scent of orange nectar

winter garden
        —rio de janeiro jardim botanico, 2009

inside this forest   /   the sky is invisible   /   all morning the rain

so many open mouths   /   palm and philodendron /   bromeliad and wren

a man and woman   /   once so drunk in love   /   find shelter here

no sound but raindrops   /   hand cupping hand   /   the moist green air

sculpture
        —bryce canyon, utah, 2007

stone asks stone   /   if thirst will tell   /   our secrets

of survival   /   a butterfly flutters   /   an old boulder blinks

just enough   /   this hardness   /   just enough wind

each stark crimson spire   /   almost cruel   /   beauty unimagined

fall's tiny harvests

when too much chill / grays November's ear / I stake my eye

path of the red / maple leaf drifting / just outside

and in my palm / five perfect petals / a Chinese hibiscus

fingers tracing / these darkened veins / the scarlet flush

cleaving

how many jabs / of madness / for this god-riven

history / a hunter's nook / orphaned teeth and toys of war

the jigsawed honing / more cheers than jeers / oh ghostly heart

all ego and gore / devoted adherents / no truer horizon

still spring

on poppy-domed hills / after the rains / pilgrims' eyes brimming

armfuls of laughter / well past dark / chatter of sparrows and kids

whose small-throated sighs / a lover's quarrel / that blue trickster time

how much more / our wide shining eyes / is this the last kiss

NOTES

Pg. 34 "36 Views of Manzanar"
nisei: second-generation Japanese American

Pg. 38 "36 Views of Manzanar"
issei: first-generation Japanese American; the generation which immigrated from Japan

Pg. 41 "36 Views of Manzanar"
Manchester Boddy was an American newspaper publisher whose estate become Descanso Gardens in La Canada, California. Descanso Gardens, now owned by Los Angeles County, contains one of North America's largest camellia collections, including the 300,000 camellias he purchased from F.M. Uyematsu.

Pg. 45 "36 Views of Manzanar"
bon odori: a traditional folk dance during obon, an August festival Buddhists observe to honor the dead

Pg. 47 "36 Views of Manzanar"
sansei: third-generation Japanese American

Pg. 51 "The Bachi-Bachi Buddhahead Blues"
Buddhahead: terms sometimes used by Japanese Americans to refer to each other
JA: Japanese American

Pg. 57 "I Wish I'd Seen My Nisei Father Dance"
yogore: tough or rowdy young men

Pg. 61   "Little Tokyo Haiku, 2019"
hapa: Hawaiian term for 'part' or 'mixed' race
Bronzeville: name for Little Tokyo during World War II when
Japanese American residents had been sent to camp and
African Americans lived there

Pg. 62   "Love-In for Jeremy Lin"
Jeremy Lin, drafted in 2010, is the second Asian American NBA player.
The little-known first Asian American and nonwhite in the NBA was
nisei Wataru Misaka in 1947.

Pg. 73   "This Tree, That Tree"
sakura: Japanese for cherry blossom tree

ACKNOWLEDGMENTS

I'm grateful to What Words Press for publishing this manuscript. Elena Karina Byrne was especially helpful in the final editing phase. In addition, I could not have written this collection without sister poets Michelle Reed, Ann Colburn, and Daria Donovan, who viewed many of the poems as they evolved. As always, my writing mentor Peter Levitt remains a presence in so much of my work. A special thanks also to Taiji Miyagawa, who has accompanied me on acoustic bass for so many of my book readings. I've enjoyed a special connection with the Ventura poetry community through poet buddies Phil Taggart and Marsha de la O. And my husband Raúl Contreras continues to encourage me in all my poetry endeavors.

I also appreciate the following literary journals and online magazines for printing many of the poems which appear in this book. *Bamboo Ridge Journal* in Hawaii has been especially supportive for the past three decades. The poems listed below were first published in the following publications:

Altadena Poetry Review 2019: "Chinese Snowballs at Huntington Gardens," "in what season love, in what season dying"

Altadena Poetry Review 2020: "How To Become a Better Noodle Poet"

Artlife: "The Basket"

Askew: "It Isn't Coincidence," "An Afternoon with Guitar Shorty"

Bamboo Ridge Journal: "Little Tokyo Haiku," "Sister Stone," "When the World Agrees on Nothing"

Cultural Weekly: "On My Way to J-Town," "The Suitcase"

Dusie: "Comfort Women"

East Wind: Politics and Culture of Asian Pacific America: "Homebound Haiku," "The Panthers"

51%: "Elder Sister"

Global Graffiti: 2 sections from "in what season love, in what season dying"

In the Grove: "Among the Containers"

Interliq: "Winter Friend, the Pine"

Kyoto Journal: "A Woman's Papers Flying in the Wind"

Lantern Review: "The Bachi-Bachi Buddhahead Blues"

Massachusetts Review: "The Older, The More"

Migrare: "Love-in for Jeremy Lin"

Miramar: "In Praise of Trust, Old School"

Narrative Magazine: "Shamisen and Straw," "This Hand"

Poetry Diversity: "None of These Women Are Smiling," "& My 5 Desires"

Rattle: "I Wish I'd Seen My Nisei Father Dance," "Zumba at 9 AM"

Rigorous: "So Are We Becoming More Visible," "Pandemic Postscript: Or Are We Too Visible Again"

Spillway: "Finding Rumi in Peru," "This Tree, That Tree," "Unrelenting This Heat / Unforgiving This July"

Would Be Saboteurs Take Heed: "Winter, 2016"

AMY UYEMATSU is a sansei (3rd-generation Japanese American) poet from Pasadena/Sierra Madre. She has five previously published collections: *Basic Vocabulary*; *The Yellow Door*; *Stone Bow Prayer*; *Nights of Fire, Nights of Rain*; and *30 Miles from J-Town*. In 1992 she won the Nicholas Roerich Poetry Prize for *30 Miles from J-Town*. Amy was a public high school math teacher for 32 years. Prior to that, she was the first Publications Coordinator for the newly established UCLA Asian American Studies Center and co-edited the widely-used anthology, *Roots: An Asian American Reader* (1971). In describing her work, the Poetry Foundation says that "Uyematsu's poems consider the intersection of politics, mathematics, spirituality, and the natural world." In 2012 Amy was recognized by the Friends of the Little Tokyo Branch Library for her writing contributions to the Japanese American community. Now retired, Amy has led writing workshops at the Far East Lounge in LA's Little Tokyo. Recent essays include "Old Asian American Poets Never Die" (*Huffington Post*, 2014) and "Five Decades Later: Reflections of a Yellow Power Advocate Turned Poet" (*Flashpoints for Asian American Studies,* 2017). Since the 1980s Amy has been performing her poetry—including the Los Angeles Times Festival of Books, the Library of Congress' National Book Festival, the Nisei Week Festival, and the Broad Museum's "L.A. Intersections: Music, Language, Movement."

www.ingramcontent.com/pod-product-compliance
Lightning Source LLC
Chambersburg PA
CBHW030451010526
44118CB00011B/883